After initially training as a nurse Anne Beech stopped work to raise her two children. She returned to work but this time in an inner city primary school. Anne really enjoyed working with the children. Reading is a vital skill and she loved helping the children to achieve their full potential. This also inspired her to write her own book based on the daily routine in a school that the children could easily relate to.

For all teachers and support staff.

Education is the key that opens the door to a brighter future.

Anne Beech

PARTNERS IN MISCHIEF

AUSTIN MACAULEY PUBLISHERS™

LONDON * CAMBRIDGE * NEW YORK * SHARJAH

A CIP catalogue record for this title is available from the British Library.

ISBN 9781528972727 (Paperback)
ISBN 9781528978415 (ePub e-book)

www.austinmacauley.com

First Published 2023
Austin Macauley Publishers Ltd®
1 Canada Square
Canary Wharf
London
E14 5AA

For my family. Thank you for your love and support.

Peter Samuels was sitting in class, staring at the door. It was maths, fractions.

2/3 + 7/12 2/3 of 9 4/8 of 16……

"Remember, the denominator has to be the same. Peter, PETER!" shouted Mrs Gordan across the room. "Look at the board. No wonder you never know what to do."

Reluctantly, Peter turned to look at Mrs Gordan. She was his class teacher. He liked her. She could be quite strict at times but she always listened to whatever you had to say. She always wore the same brown jacket, regardless of the weather. Her hair was a mass of thick, wavy curls that never looked like she brushed them. He had no idea how old she was.

About 60, he thought.

Some children said she was almost 90 because she had been at that school forever. He repressed the urge to answer her back and pretended to pay attention.

¾ of 16 4/8 of 325/6+3/9…… The lesson continued along these lines.

Every 10 minutes or so, he raised his head and glanced towards the door. Hopefully, the door would stick shut. He didn't really think that this would happen, but you never know!

"Oh, what's goin' on?" Tom flicked Peter's ear. The sharp pain caused him to jerk upright and bang his knee sharply on the table.

"What's up with you today? Is it the football? You didn't come to breakfast club this morning. I had to sit next to that new kid Harrison. He's weird. And why do you keep looking at the door?"

<h1 style="text-align:center">1</h1>

Tom Sanderson was Peter's best friend and buddy in all his adventures. They had known each other since they started school on the same day in nursery. Peter realised he was a good friend when Sally Crosby stole his teddy, refused to give it back and Tom had pushed her over into the sandpit and returned Tatty bear without a single word.

"Nothing. I was just late. Slept in.. Peter didn't want to look at Tom, as he knew his face would show it wasn't the truth. Before Tom could reply…

"Make sure you finish the last question. Leave your books in a neat pile and get ready for playtime." Mrs Gordan's soft voice floated through the air. Surprisingly, over the sound of chair legs scrapping on the floor, the gossiping chatter of the table of six silly girls at the back (or the fluffy heads, as Peter and Tom called them) her voice was heard and everyone did what was expected of them.

The classroom back door into the playground was Peter's escape route. Normally, he would hang about in the corridor, either hoping Tobias Watts had brought in his usual supply of chocolate or swapping around the P.E. kits of the silly gang of six. But not today. He was first out. He legged it as fast and as far as he could. Tom's shouting faded into the distance. He ran, panting hard, out of breath, his heart pounding in his chest. He sat down on the cold playground floor. His eyes scanned the playground. Which teachers were on duty today? Ah, Mr Gibbs. He was the Year 3 teacher, and Mrs O'Sullivan, who was a supply teacher covering Mr Woods' class.

He didn't know why Mr Woods wasn't there today but he didn't care.

"There you are." Tom appeared, red-faced and, to Peter's shame, a little upset.

"Is it me? What have I done?"

"Nothing. No, it's not you. I'll explain later but not now." Peter didn't want to talk but he didn't want to upset Tom either.

"Come on, let's find Tobias. He's got biscuits today." He distracted Tom with the thought of illegal food; they were only supposed to have fruit as a snack.

Peter was convinced the teachers knew about the food Tobias brought in. Perhaps he brought them treats as well. The staff room always seemed to have biscuits and cakes on the table. You could just see them if you peered through the small glass panel in the door.

For the next 10 minutes, the crumbly chocolate delights of choco crisps distracted Peter from his worries but when the sharp trill of the whistle blew, he tensed up again.

Only one and a half hours to go until lunch. Perhaps I can pretend to be ill and hide in the toilets, he thought.

To get back to his classroom, he had to walk past the office, past the staffroom and… past the head teacher's office. That was the problem.

Luckily, Summer Brown had a fluffy blue coat with a massive hood. It was hideous, and normally Peter would have something to say about that, but not today. It acted as a screen to hide behind as long as he kept close to her. He pretended to see a spider on it, causing her to screech and cry. Offering to get rid of the insect gave him a good excuse to hide behind her. He was soon back outside his classroom.

Good, he thought, *that worked…*

"Peter, can I see you at lunchtime, please?"

That was not good. He recognised that voice, the one person he had managed to avoid all morning, the head teacher, Mr Turner. His heart sank. He turned slowly to face the one person he really, REALLY didn't want to see.

"Straight after English, please, Peter. Don't be late." And then he was gone back into his office. How can so few words make you feel so terrible?

"What does Turner want?" asked Morrice, peering over the top of his thick, rimmed glasses.

"None of your business," snapped back Peter.

English was a blur. Poems, not Peter's best subject. Why did they have to use similes anyway? Hot as the sun, quick as a flash, black as coal. All Peter heard was blah, blah, blah!

"Come on, Peter, you're not with it today, are you?" Mrs Gordan's observation was correct.

"As hopeless as the school football team," chirped up Melissa from the back table. Her little group of friends sniggered together.

"Shut up!" shouted Tom, as always defending his friend.

"That's enough. Finish your work in silence now." Mrs Gordan walked around the classroom, the heels of her bright blue shoes clicking on the hard floor. After what seemed like an eternity, finally English was over.

"Books here please. Toilet, wash hands and line up for lunch. Apart from you, Peter. I think Mr Turner wants to see you."

There was no escape. It was time.

2

He took a deep breath and knocked on the door.

"Oooo, what have you done?" a cheeky-faced boy, who Peter thought was in Year 2, stared at him, grinning as he walked past.

"Come in."

He turned the cold brass handle and entered the head teacher's office. Peter had been here many times. Some for good reasons and some for others! Putting glue in Scott Windsor's hair was one of them.

Mr Turner stood behind his desk, looking out of the window into the playground, watching the children running, skipping and jumping around. Peter longed to be there as well. "Well, Peter, this is tricky, isn't it?"

You can say that again, Peter thought to himself. *YOU made it tricky, not me.*

"Have you spoken to your mother at all? I haven't said anything to Kathy yet. I wondered if you had."

Hearing the head teacher refer to his mum by her first name made Peter's skin feel suddenly feel cold all over. It wasn't a nice feeling.

"No, I haven't," he replied quietly.

The truth was that yesterday evening, Peter had seen Mr Turner leaving his house. He had been laughing, smiling and, and—Peter swallowed hard—he was holding his mum's hand, and just before he left and got into his car, he KISSED HER. He shouldn't have seen this. He was supposed to be at Tom's house watching the FA cup semi-final between United and City.

Tom's dog, Butch, had somehow jumped up onto the table and knocked over the TV when Tom had thrown Peter's scarf across the room. This had caused a major row in Tom's house, so Peter had decided to go home. He ran the two blocks in world-record speed so not to miss the free kick United had just been awarded. He should have rung Mum first, but in his excitement, he had forgotten.

As he turned the corner into his road, he noticed something familiar. A large jeep, army-green, with a United sticker in the back window.

That's strange, Peter had thought, *it looks just like Mr Turner's car.*

Everyone at school knew his car; it was really cool because it looked just like the one in the new Xbox game, Army Convoy.

Hang on, it *was* his car. There could only be one car with the same battered bumper, Union jack air-freshener hanging from the mirror and the registration number BU12POO. (It was a great joke at school that it almost spelt out I want to poo!) *What's it doing here?* He slowed down to a very slow walk, having completely forgotten about the United free kick.

At that point, his front door opened, and out had come his mum and Mr Turner, laughing, smiling and HOLDING HANDS. Peter had quickly jumped behind the bins, that luckily for him Fred at number 20 had only an hour earlier put out for collection. He stayed there crouched down low, watching their every move. It was then he saw the KISS. The image still hurt him when he thought about it.

He thought he was well hidden until Mr Turner drove away. Just as he turned the corner, their eyes met! It must only have been for a second but to Peter, and probably Mr Turner as well, it had seemed like a lifetime. Mr Turner's expression changed from a happy, childlike grin—singing along to the cheesy music mix he often played—to suddenly the face of someone caught stealing cookies from the biscuit tin. A guilty, stunned look!

He repeated, this time louder, "No, I haven't."

"You didn't speak to your mum when you got in yesterday?" Mr Turner asked. This time, he was looking straight at him, a bead of sweat about to run from his forehead down his nose and onto the desk below.

"No, I said I was tired and went straight to bed. I pretended I had fallen out with Tom over the football and didn't want to talk. This morning, Mum had to leave earlier than normal. She had to collect a parcel from the post office before she went to work." His mum worked at the local supermarket, and every Saturday evening, she would bring home cakes and pies that hadn't been sold and were past their use by date. Sunday lunch and tea were always amazing, which probably explained why Tom always seemed to turn up mid-afternoon and wasn't very keen on leaving! Peter's mum had a soft spot for Tom since the Tatty bear incident in nursery, so she never seemed to mind when he turned up and needed feeding.

She had checked he was up and dressed before she left and made him promise that he would brush his teeth and lock up before he left for breakfast club. She had seemed very chirpy that morning, singing along to the radio. She kissed him on the head and was gone.

How could she! Mr Turner of all people. Peter had hoped it was all a bad dream and that when he woke up, everything would be back to normal. His morning had got worse when his phone beeped repeatedly, a message from Tom.

'2 − 0, 2 − 0, 2 − 0. See you later, loser!'

That must have meant that City had won the football. Tom was a massive city supporter and would not give up any chance of boasting about them beating United.

He had left the house on time but had no intention of going to breakfast club. He had grabbed a packet of crisps out of the cupboard and munched them slowly as he walked the long way to school, carefully avoiding any routes where he thought he might bump into Tom, or worse, Mr Turner. He spent the next 20 minutes trying to work things out in his head.

Mr Turner was okay. In fact, up until then, Peter liked him. He was strict if you were naughty but he was also fair. He was also a successful teacher. Since he had been at Cameron Street Primary School, the SATs results had dramatically improved.

He loved football. Last summer when the World Cup was on, the school had regular mufti days. You could wear a football shirt or a t-shirt that was red, white or blue instead of school uniform. The England matches that were during the school day. The World Cup was over in Japan and the matches were put on in the main hall on the big screen.

As long as your teacher said you had done all your work, you were allowed to go along and watch. The atmosphere had been amazing, especially when England beat Germany 2 – 1 and Brooks (a United player) scored the winning goal. In his office, Mr Turner had a football sticker book. Twice a week, the staff chose one child from each class—whose behaviour or work had improved—to open a packet of stickers and stick them in the book. When the sticker book was complete, the staff would vote for one child to win the whole thing.

Peter and Tom had tried so hard during that time. Tom got chosen for learning his 8x tables but Peter had missed out. At first, he felt really jealous but deep down, he knew Tom had deserved it; he had always struggled in maths. The winner of the sticker book was a girl! Sarah Fleetman in Y6. The teachers had thought that her attitude in helping others; especially the younger ones was an example to all.

Peter knew he wouldn't win the book, but to make it worse, he heard that she didn't really like football and had given the book to her older sister's boyfriend.

Mr Turner also had a big tin on his desk. In it was a mass of stickers, rubbers, pencils and lots of other little treats. Whenever a child was sent to him for good behaviour, exceptional work or if they were really upset about something, the big tin would be opened and the child was allowed to choose out of it. In Y4, Peter had fallen over in the playground and had badly twisted his ankle. Whilst waiting to go home, he had chosen a United pencil and rubber.

The big tin now stood between him and the teacher who kissed his mum. Arrghh!! Mr Turner has kissed *his* mum. He still couldn't believe it.

"I was going to ring Kathy but thought I would clear the air with you first."

Peter didn't know what to say. He sat staring at the tin. His stomach started to rumble, and he realised he was suddenly really hungry, even though he had eaten three choco crisps at playtime. "Can I go to lunch, please?"

"Peter, we really need to talk about this. Your mum and I are really good friends and I care about her. We've wanted to tell you for ages."

For ages! What did that mean? Peter looked up from the tin to meet Mr Turner's gaze.

I could stare him out, he thought for a brief moment. "What do you mean for ages? How long have you been seeing my mum?" he whispered in a croaky voice.

"I think that's up to her to talk about with you but I want you to know that we intend to spend more time together in the future. I hope this won't change things between us at school. Go to lunch now and speak to your mum at home." He couldn't get out of there quick enough. The dinner lady called to him down the corridor to get into lunch quickly before it was all gone.

3

The rest of the afternoon was a blur. Tom had wanted to re-enact the goals from last night's game at lunchtime but Peter managed to get out of it by offering to help clear the lunch table away, earning himself two house points in doing so.

The afternoon lesson was art. The Romans. He had been really looking forward to this. Romans were this term's topic, and today they were going to make swords and shields for the Roman Day workshop that was planned for next week. But today it had lost its appeal. Miss Johnson, the art teacher, helped him cut the thick cardboard to the right length.

"What's up, Petey?" she whispered to him. Normally, he would reply, "I'm not called Petey." But today, he just let it go.

"Nothing, miss." She moved away to break up a disagreement between Max and David, who had both decided they both needed the last piece of thick cardboard.

"You going to tell me yet?" It was Tom. "Sorry if I teased you about the football but United normally wins, so I couldn't resist."

"Just stuff at home," Peter replied. "Meet me after school at the swings and I'll tell you all about it."

"Okay." Tom seemed happy with his reply and returned to splashing red paint over his carefully designed creation.

Soon, it was home time. Grabbing his coat from his peg, Peter pushed past the silly girls with their glittery matching backpacks and headed for the main door.

Luckily, Y5 were allowed to walk home without having to wait for an adult to collect them. He was so glad that he had that extra time to think before he saw his mum.

At first, he walked slowly, trying to delay the inevitable but after a while, he decided it was best to get it over with. Picking up his pace, he soon reached his street. He could imagine his mum stood in the kitchen, wearing her bake-off apron (a Christmas present from Auntie Jenny) washing the dishes that would be left over from the night before.

As he opened the door—silence. Normally, the radio would be on and music would be filling the air. Today no music. She wasn't in the kitchen and he could see the apron folded up on the worktop surface.

"Peter, there you are. I was starting to worry." Her voice, quiet and soft, came from the lounge. She was sat on the sofa perched uncomfortably on the edge. "Come and sit down." She patted the cushions next to her. He did as he was asked, trying hard not to make eye contact. It was obvious that she knew. Mr Turner must have rung her. Her manner was so different to how she was this morning.

"I'm sorry; I didn't mean for you to find out like this. When Alan—"

Oh God! Alan, Alan Turner. Peter looked at the floor.

"—When Alan said you saw him last night, I was devastated. I know this is difficult for you, and I really wanted to tell you myself. He's a good, kind man and I really like him." A long pause followed. What could he say?

"How long have you been seeing him for, and when did you meet?" Peter blurted out, finally looking his mum in the face.

"I've known Alan." Alan again! He hated hearing teachers being called by their first names, especially Mr Turner. "I've known him since you started school, but it was at Christmas that we became friendly. Remember, I offered to help at the school fair. We started to talk and soon became friends. I know it's hard for you to understand."

"I'm not a baby!" Peter shouted out indignantly. "I know how boyfriends and girlfriends work. It's just that it's *him*."

His mum continued, "No one will ever replace your father, but I get lonely, and Alan is so funny and makes me laugh and feel happy."

My father. Peter's dad had died when he was three years old—a car accident caused by some oil spilt on the road by another car. Peter didn't really remember him. There were loads of photos of them together, at the football, (He was a mad United fan, of course.) at Christmas and on their yearly holiday to Wales. Peter had his dad's football shirt above his bed. He suddenly felt guilty that he couldn't remember him. He did remember, however, his mum crying, looking sad and constantly worrying about money and the cost of everything.

"You are my world, pumpkin."

Oh no. She's started to call me pumpkin again.

Pumpkin was his mum's pet name for him, and she always used it in times of illness or another crisis. "I promise that you come first, but please give Alan a chance."

Peter thought a change of subject would be good. "What's for tea? Can we have chips?"

The distraction worked. Chips, beans and sausages followed by chocolate cheesecake. They sat in silence at the table, opposite each other, rarely looking up from their plates. Normally, teatime would by a loud, noisy time, Mum asking about school and Peter filling her in about all the things the silly girls did and who was in trouble that day. However, this evening was very different. When every trace of chocolate had left the bowl, Peter announced that he was off to see Tom. "I won't be late." He grabbed his jacket from the bottom of the stairs, where he had thrown it when he came in, and opened the front door. He could feel his mum's eyes watching him.

"Love you, pumpkin," she whispered as he slammed the door shut.

4

As usual, Tom was at the park first. This time, he had Butch with him. He was a small, scruffy-looking dog with big, floppy ears, one of which always seemed to be sticking up at a strange angle. Peter liked Butch. He had known him for a long time and a small part of him was jealous of the relationship Tom had with him. Butch was completely loyal and dedicated to Tom, and if anyone showed any anger or bad will to Tom, his faithful servant was straight away by his side to defend his master. He recognised Peter, as the boys spent so much time together, and his little, stubby tail wagged so fast at the sight of him that Peter thought for one second, Butch would take off like a helicopter.

"Mum made me bring him, especially after last night." Tom yanked gently on the lead as Butch tried to jump up and lick Peter's face.

"How's the TV?" Peter asked.

"Luckily, no real damage or this one," Tom nodded his head towards Butch, "would have been out!" Butch suddenly gave a little whimper as if he knew he was being talked about.

Giving Peter a sharp poke on the arm, Tom turned to look at him straight in the face and demanded, "Are you going to tell me now what's going on?" It was obvious that Tom would not take no for an answer.

They sat on the swings, glaring menacingly at any children who came close, and Peter told Tom everything.

Tom's facial expressions changed several times from shock, amazement and finally disgust as Peter described the kiss. After 10 minutes of talking, several minutes of silence, a loud 'OMG' and a sudden, shrill burst of laughter came from Tom's gaping mouth. "Mr Turner and your mum! Alan and Kathy! OMG. What, since Christmas!" Needless to say, Tom was as surprised and horrified as Peter had been. "Kissing? How disgusting. Did you have a nightmare last night? Oooooo, imagine if they got married, you would become Peter Turner."

"Okay, that's enough," Peter interrupted abruptly.

"Seriously, what are we going to do?" Tom finally became calm and serious.

"We?" questioned Peter.

"Yes, we. We are a team. Remember, no one hurts or upsets my mate." Tom placed a comforting arm around Peter's shoulder.

That was the golden question. What could be done? What was he going to do? What could he possibly do without hurting the most important person in his life?

"I've no idea," he replied as Tom slid off the swing, rubbing his bottom. Butch was pulling frantically at his lead as he spotted a cat on the grass bank nearby. Tom's phone suddenly bleeped loudly, causing both the boys to jump with surprise. It was his mum demanding he come home now to finish his chores.

"I'd better go. See you at breakfast club tomorrow and we'll try and work out a plan." With a nod, Tom and Butch ran out of the park and up the hill to the estate where they lived.

Peter knew he could trust Tom to not tell anyone but to make sure, he texted him to swear to silence. Tom replied with a big thumbs-up.

When Peter got home, his mum was sitting cross-legged on the sofa, watching her favourite soap. As usual, the characters were arguing. Why she liked this rubbish so much, Peter had no idea. As he entered the room, she turned the TV to mute. "Suppose you spoke to Tom and told him?"

"Yes, but don't worry, your secret is safe. Tom won't tell anyone; he's a good mate." Peter looked at her directly and was shocked to see that her eyes were red and blotchy. She had been crying.

She held out her hand, and in a moment of spontaneity, they hugged tightly. Peter suddenly felt guilty. He loved his mum so much; how could he do or say anything that would make her unhappy?

As his mum went to sit back down on the sofa, she softly whispered,

"It will be fine, pumpkin, I promise. Please give Alan a chance."

He gave his mum a kiss on the cheek and told her he was really tired and was off to bed. He was halfway up the stairs when he suddenly stopped. He could hear her talking.

"Yes, I've spoken to him. I know, but what can we do? He's told Tom, Tom Sanderson. Peter's a sensible boy, so hopefully he will come around. Okay, see you tomorrow? Love you too, bye."

She had been talking to him. Love you too—urgh. He'll come around! As he entered his bedroom, Peter was thinking. *This couldn't go on.*

He decided he needed to stop this. Exhausted, he collapsed onto his bed and was soon fast asleep. For one brief moment when he awoke, it seemed like a normal weekday, but then reality soon dawned on him.

5

He quickly got dressed into his school uniform and rushed out of the front door. He somehow had managed to avoid seeing his mum. She was spending ages in her bedroom straightening her hair—probably for Alan! That thought had managed to refocus him on the fact that he needed to do something. He wasn't too worried as he was sure that he and Tom would be able to come up with a good plan.

When he arrived at school, Tom had already devoured two large bowls of cereal and was munching on jam-covered toast. A trail of crumbs showing everyone where he had been. Peter clutched his bowl of hot sticky porridge—school porridge was amazing—and went to find him. In between slurps of porridge and crunches of toast, the two friends started to make a plan.

"You can't allow a teacher to go out with your mum. It's not right, it's weird! What if he moved in? School at school and school at home. Fractions at breakfast, nouns for lunch and square roots for tea!" Tom had said all that in one big breath whilst also licking the jam off his fingers. He knew it was an exaggeration, but Peter knew what Tom was getting at.

"I know," replied Peter. "But what can we do about it?" That was the obvious but difficult question.

Every chance the boys got, they would sit together in a huddle, trying to come up with an idea. Tom's ideas ranged from ringing the police to get Mr Turner arrested for speeding, putting a sausage in his car exhaust pipe to putting one of Butch's poos in his big tin!

Apart from the sausage idea, none of them were really any good. They had no proof of the speeding, and who in their right minds would want to pick up Butch's poos, let alone carry it to school!?

At lunch, it was strangely sausage and mash on the menu. Peter took this as a sign, so he decided as a joke to keep one of his sausages. He carefully slid it off his plate, wrapping it in a paper towel and pushing it into his pocket when the dinner lady went to mop up the mess a Year 1 had made. The same child also decided to have a temper tantrum, throwing himself onto the floor, screaming for his mum. The boys used this opportunity to sneak out of the dinner hall and into the staff car park.

With Tom keeping watch by the backdoor, Peter crept over to Mr Turner's jeep. Taking the cold, slimy gravy-coated Cumberland out of his now sticky pocket, Peter slowly and carefully pushed it as far as he could up the exhaust pipe. Once done, he signalled to Tom a quick thumbs-up, and the two boys legged it as fast as they could back into the bustling playground, hoping no one had missed them. After a quick high-five of congratulations, the two boys joined in a game of football. United against Argyle. United won, of course. For the first time in what seemed like an eternity, Peter felt content.

Unfortunately for them, they had both forgotten that the school and the car park were all covered by CCTV.

Twenty minutes before the end of the day, just as the class was finishing off, their science experiments—recording how shadows were formed and how the movement of the sun affected them—Mrs Gordan called out across the room.

"Oh, Peter and Tom, sorry I completely forgot, silly me. Can you pop down to Mr Turner's office, please? He needed to have a word with you both. I hope you two haven't been up to no good." She gave a little chuckle at the thought.

These words stunned them both. They turned their heads slowly to face each other. The colour had completely drained from Tom's face, causing him to look a strange ghostly grey. Without speaking a word, they put down their pencils and books and, as slowly as they could possibly go, went into the corridor.

As soon as the classroom door closed, Tom swallowed hard. "We're done for now. Mum will kill me. I'll be grounded forever. Oh God, what will Dad say?"

"Shut up. He doesn't know it was us, does he? No one saw us, did they?" Peter hoped he sounded convincing but he was also really worried.

For the second time in two days, Peter was yet again, although this time with a companion, stood outside the head teacher's office door.

6

"Well, well, well, boys. I'm a bit disappointed. I thought Peter, or hoped, that we could try and be friends. Tom, I know you two are good friends and that he has told you about our situation but really, a sausage!?"

"But how did—"

Before Tom could finish, Mr Turner pointed to the TV screen in the corner of his office. On it, on pause was a picture of Peter with his finger up the exhaust pipe of the jeep and Tom stood nearby on lookout.

Flip, thought Peter. A basic error. He had forgotten all about the CCTV. The cameras were all over school, so how could the boys have not thought about them!? The question was what was going to happen now. Peter could sense Tom's worry. For all his friends talked about being brave and breaking rules, he was more worried about his mum and dad's reaction.

Surprisingly, Alan did nothing.

"Look, boys. I'm prepared to ignore this silly prank if you two promise to leave it at that. I won't even tell your parents. Have a think about your behaviour and let that be the end of it. Peter, I don't want to worry your mother over this, so let's try and get on."

Tom let out a sigh of relief and looked disbelievingly at his friend.

"Thanks, Alan," Peter replied cheekily as they both hurried out the door before Mr Turner had a chance to change his mind.

Walking home together, kicking an empty cola can along the pavement, the boys were wondering what on Earth they could do next. Tom said that he could still get Butch to do his business but Peter thought that a silly and smelly plan. They needed something better, something that would really affect Mr Turner. It had to be a plan that stopped him seeing Peter's mum for good. What was the most important thing for teachers, especially head teachers?

"Maths, spellings, tests, science," Tom was just saying any lesson that came into his head.

"Hang on a minute." Peter stopped suddenly in his tracks. "Year 6 SATs are the most important thing to all teachers, especially head teachers. Remember how in assembly he is always going on about Y6. Be nice to them. It's a very important year. These results mean so much, etc. etc. What if we could do something about them?"

Tom smiled cheekily. He hated tests, any tests, and would do anything to get out of them.

Tomorrow was Friday, so they had two days to plan things.

Ruin the school SATs and Mr Turner would be sacked, would have to move away and life would go back to normal.

Friday at school passed quietly. Peter reverted to his normal hobby of swapping the silly girls PE kits around and denying all knowledge of it. Tobias brought in *Maltesers*, although by break time, they had melted into a sticky mess.

Apart from assembly, neither Tom nor Peter saw Mr Turner. Even then, they avoided eye contact with him. One thing that did get Peter's attention was Mrs O'Sullivan in Y2. Every time Mr Turner spoke, she seemed to tut to herself or shake her head. When Y6 were mentioned, the usual be-nice-to-them talk; she seemed to let out a little quiet laugh. This seemed very strange!

Tom and Peter had arranged to meet by the swings, the place where all their adventures usually began, on Saturday at 10 a.m.

Feeling a little happier, Peter ran home, hoping he could get a couple of hours on army convoy before he was made to get off the Xbox. He had neglected the game this week and was behind a boy called Superman Fred 37 by 1000 points in the league table.

As he opened the front door, he was pleased to see Mum in her bake-off apron, standing in the kitchen.

"Hello, love, okay?"

"Yes, thanks Mum," he replied, grabbing an apple and running upstairs to his room before she could ask any more questions about his day at school.

After 30 minutes of chasing army trucks around Africa, and only 50 points behind Superman Fred, Mum knocked on his door.

"Peter, how about we go out for pizza tonight? I think we deserve it, don't you? Be ready in 10 minutes."

His first instinct was to say, "No, I need to finish this game," but he loved the local pizza bar. Double pepperoni and chicken with added mushrooms.

"Okay, I'll be down in a minute." He just had time to destroy two super trucks and take over the leader board before he signed off. Feeling happy and content, the first time in a while, he grabbed his favourite jacket from the wardrobe and headed downstairs. Top of the leader board, pizza and meeting Tom tomorrow gave Peter a cause to smile.

However, his mood soon changed!

7

"Hello, Peter."

"I hope you don't mind love, but I invited Alan. I thought we should have a chat and sort things out." Peter's mum ruffled his hair, kissed him on the top of his head and pushed him out the door before he had a chance to change his mind.

Last week, if Mr Turner had given him a lift in his jeep, he would have been delighted. The vehicle was exactly like the one Major Hudson of the West African Peace Corps drove, except it didn't have machineguns strapped to the back of it.

The adults chatted happily in the front as they drove into town but Peter crouched down as low as he could in the back, just in case he was seen by anyone he knew. The teasing he would get would be off the scale if anyone knew!

Pizza Palace was Peter's favourite place to eat—but not today. The deluxe pizza special was dry and tasteless. Even the two large colas he had couldn't rid his mouth of the coarse, peppery flavour they had left behind. It wasn't really the pizza—Peter knew that; it was the company. Sat opposite, he watched the two adults talk, laugh, share a joke and occasionally turn and smile at him. He knew what they were doing. Acting normal, hoping he would just fall into line. He couldn't take any more.

"Didn't you think of me at all?" Peter blurted out, almost choking on a piece of spicy sausage. "If it gets out, I'll be the laughing stock of the school. Why him, Mum? Why him?"

The atmosphere around the table had suddenly changed.

"That's enough. Don't speak to your mother like that." Mr Turner suddenly looked serious. Peter had seen that expression many times before.

"We're not at school now. You can't put me in detention!"

"That's enough." His mum banged the table with her fist, "We didn't deliberately set out to upset you, but it's not all about you. I have a life too. Before this, I know you liked Alan, so please just give him a chance; and there's no need to be rude."

For the rest of the meal, Peter chose the silent treatment, refusing to join in any conversation or make any eye contact with his mum. He did, however, text Tom to update him on things.

'OMG, WHAT? NO WAY,' were just some of Tom's replies.

The rest of the evening passed without any more drama. Peter, still refusing to talk got in the jeep, got out the jeep, went into the house, watched TV and then went to bed.

His mum had tried, for a while, to talk to him but she knew that he could be very stubborn, so by bedtime, she had given up. She just shouted up to him, "Night, pumpkin! Love you."

8

Saturday morning, Mum didn't work weekends, so normally they would have breakfast together and chat. On special occasions, she would make pancakes. He could smell them this morning as he was getting dressed.

Oh no, she trying to bribe me with food, he thought.

As he walked into the kitchen, the sweet smell of the pancakes filled the air, making his mouth water.

"I thought we could—"

"Sorry, Mum," Peter interrupted, "I'm meeting Tom and I'm already late." He grabbed two sticky, hot pancakes from the pan and rushed out of the kitchen before she could reply. Part of him felt guilty. He knew she was trying really hard. *Ouch,* the pancakes were hotter than he had thought, but the head teacher—no way! He wiped the sticky goo on his fingers over his jeans, forced the two delicious pancakes into his mouth and ran off to the park to meet up with Tom, the only person who really understood what he was going through.

Tom was sat in the middle of the playing field, bouncing a blue football between his legs. He made Peter repeat everything about last night. He particularly wanted to know about the jeep. He agreed that although he would really like to ride in the jeep, it was totally out of order for Mr Turner to be at Pizza Palace. Following a quick game of City V United which was a draw—every time they played, it had to be a draw to stop any arguments—they sat down behind the goal to start their plan.

At first, breathing heavily, they had just played a cup final. They just sat looking at each other. Then slowly, ideas started to develop.

What's the best way to disrupt the SATs?

Steal the papers! Not possible, as they were always locked away in the school safe.

Burn down the school! A bit too drastic, they decided, especially as they both didn't want to destroy the Roman shields and swords they had only just finished making.

Kidnap Mr Wallace, the Y6 teacher! They would only replace him with someone else and where would they keep him anyway.

Spread a rumour that Mr Turner was a Russian spy!

Put something icky in the Y6 school dinners so they were not well enough to take the tests. What could they use? And the SATs were all week, not just one day.

After 15 minutes of these and other silly ideas, the boys were no further on.

Changing the subject dramatically, Tom suddenly flicked Peter's ear. "Is that Mrs O'Sullivan from Year 2 over there?" he said, pointing to the playfield car park.

It was. She was standing next to a large white van, talking to a strange-looking man in a dark jacket. Although they were almost a whole football pitch away, the boys could tell it was a serious conversation. They decided to investigate what was going on. They also needed a break from thinking too hard about what they were going to do.

9

They jogged around the edge of the pitch and carefully and slowly crept up between the two cars directly opposite the white van.

"Yes, I know! It's not easy they all love him, although I've no idea why. Okay."

They couldn't hear the man's voice at all, but luckily for them, Mrs O'Sullivan had a loud, booming voice which proved very useful in her class at school. The Year 2 class was well known for being the noisiest and most disruptive group of children in the building.

"I do know something useful. He is dating the mum of one of the children in Year 5. Peter Samuels he's called. Yep, okay. I'll keep you updated. I do miss Oakside, you know. It's just not the same at Cameron Street."

At the sound of his name, Peter had suddenly felt a strange sickly feeling in the pit of his stomach.

Why was she talking about him and his mum? What did Oakside School have to do with it?

The boys backed out carefully from between the cars. They crouched down low behind the large dustbins and watched as Mrs O'Sullivan waved to the mysterious man and walked away towards town.

The boys just stared at each other for what seemed like ages.

"How does she know about you and your mum and Mr Turner? Why is she talking to someone else about it? And Oakside? It's so weird."

Tom had just expressed out loud everything that Peter had been thinking.

Oakside was another primary school on the far side of town. It was a school set in beautiful woodland with large oak trees around the edge of its playing field. One of the trees even had a tree house built into it. It had beautiful flowerbeds by the entrance and hanging baskets all around the outside of the classrooms. It was very popular with parents. The waiting list was said to be five years! Chrissie West, the last winner of x-factor had gone there as a child. Her picture was all over the corridors.

Recently, however, their popularity had plummeted. Usually on top of the league tables, they were now in 5th place. Cameron Street had beaten them three years in a row, in fact, since Mr Turner had arrived.

Tom flicked Peter's ear again. "Ouch! I wish you would stop doing that."

Peter had slowly been working it all out. Mrs Sullivan's arrival, her attitude and comments in assembly and now this.

"She's a spy. She's a spy sent from Oakside." Peter jumped up so quickly when he said this that Tom was almost knocked over backwards.

Tom looked very confused. "What?"

Peter then started to try and explain, and as he did, it all seemed to make sense.

"Wow, a real spy at our school. But what's it got to do with you?" Peter was trying to think of a good answer when his thoughts were interrupted by his phone suddenly ringing.

It was his mum. He couldn't face speaking to her at this moment, so he let it go to voicemail.

"Peter, I'm going out for a few hours with Alan. I will be back in time for tea. Love you." At least she didn't call him pumpkin, but the word 'Alan' reminded him of his main problem.

Suddenly, Tom grabbed Peter's arm, squeezing so tightly that it almost made him cry out.

"Perhaps Mrs O'Sullivan could do us a favour as well. She obviously doesn't like Mr Turner. We should try and find out what she wants and if she can help us. It's worth a try, isn't it?" They sat down on the grassy bank overlooking the football pitch whilst they both tried to decide on a plan to investigate another teacher at their school.

It would prove a difficult challenge. Their classroom was on the ground floor whilst Year 2 was upstairs. There was no real reason why any child from Year 5 would need to go up there. Except to run errands for staff or the library that was upstairs. Both Tom and Peter hated reading. They were always getting moaned at by Mrs Gordan and every teacher they had ever had to read more. Reading is an important skill, a vital life skill that you would take with you through life. The boys knew this but they still had no interest in picking up a book, unless it was about sport especially football. Books were so boring.

That thought suddenly gave Peter an idea but he knew Tom wouldn't like it.

"We need to read more. Every time we change a book, we can spy on Sully." Peter had instantly given her a nickname. Tom burst out laughing, as it reminded him of the monster in a Disney film.

"I suppose it might work and it might give me some brownie points with mum. I need to keep her happy after the TV incident with Butch." Tom didn't protest as much as Peter thought he would. It was indeed a strange day.

They agreed on this plan. They walked together along the footpath to the end of James Street, talking about the upcoming football internationals. These were the only football matches that they could both talk about without disagreeing.

"I've got to go to gran's tomorrow, so will have to see you on Monday." Tom patted his best friend on the back and, with a little wave, he disappeared around the corner.

Peter walked slowly home, distracted by the football results that were popping up on his phone. *Yes! United had won again, 2 − 0, and guess who scored? Brooks, he was amazing!* His joy didn't last very long, as when he turned the corner into his street, he saw the jeep parked up on his drive.

Not again. Don't I get a weekend off from him? They better not kiss in front of me or I'll be sick.

Opening the door slowly, he tried to creep in without anyone noticing.

"I see United won again. That's great news, isn't it?" Mr Turner was trying to make small talk.

Peter snapped back, "Of course it's good news. I don't want them to lose, do I?"

"Don't be rude, Peter." Mum appeared out of the kitchen, wiping her hands on a towel. She was wearing her bake-off apron, and lovely chocolaty smells were filling the house.

"Sorry," Peter said, although he didn't really mean it. "We saw Sully, I mean Mrs O'Sullivan, in the park earlier." Peter thought he was being clever. "How long is she staying at our school?"

"Just until Mr Woods is better. He broke his ankle falling off a ladder. It's been a couple of weeks now, so he should soon be back, although he might he might need a walking stick for a while." Mr Turner went on to describe why he had been up a ladder, and at one point, Mum was laughing with him at something that must have been funny. Peter had given up listening until Sully's name was mentioned again. "She's a really keen member of staff and has been so interested in helping prepare for the SATs."

I bet she has. Peter smiled to himself. This was the longest conversation the two of them had had in ages. That's probably why his mum ruffled his hair and kissed him on the top of his head before she returned to the kitchen.

"Tea won't be long," she whispered in his ear.

10

Much to his mum's delight and Mr Turner's surprise, Peter was very chatty during their meal. He asked many questions about reading and school, especially why Cameron Street was so good at getting Year 6 through the dreaded SATs. Mum was particularly pleased when he told her he had decided to enter the reading challenge set every term by Mr Jones. Fifteen books in 10 weeks! Peter told them it would be easy but deep down he knew he would probably struggle. He could read quite well but just wasn't interested. Also two weeks had already passed. So, it was 15 books in eight weeks!

He spent most of the next day playing Army Convoy. He was way ahead on the leader board but with some serious reading coming up, he needed to get some quality gaming time in. At least no Alan today, although he did hear his mum giggling on the phone and she went all red and embarrassed when he went downstairs to get a sandwich. He tried to block any thought of the two of them together from his mind. On his way upstairs, he glimpsed something shiny out of the corner of his eye. Through the crack in the door to the lounge, he could just make out a mug placed on the mantelpiece. As he walked in the room, he realised it was the mug Mr Turner had been drinking from last night. He had put it down right in front of the picture of Peter, his mum and more importantly his dad on holiday in Wales.

Peter was sat high up on his dad's shoulders, laughing. Mum had taken the picture with a selfie stick, so she had a funny expression as she was trying to push the photo click button. Peter, to his shame, didn't often think of his dad but this made him really angry. Was Mr Turner trying to take his dad's place? Not if he could help it.

Monday morning, Peter awoke feeling determined and ready for battle. He left the house feeling confident and was looking forward to meeting Tom in breakfast club. As he approached the school gates, he began to feel uneasy. Why was Sarah Dobbs staring at him so intently from the car window as she drove past?

All of a sudden, he felt a tap on his shoulder. The fluffy heads, well two of them, were grinning at him. *What do they want?* he thought. He soon found out.

"Well, Peter, what's all this then?"

"What's what?" he replied, becoming increasingly puzzled.

Then in perfect unison, they began to sing…

"Peter's mum and Mr T KISSING." They repeated this several times, getting louder with every breath.

NO! What? This can't be happening. Peter's secret was out.

11

Peter turned and screamed in their faces. "Shut up. You don't know anything." Trying hard to stop himself from crying, he turned and ran into school to get as far away from them as possible. How did they know? If they knew, then everyone would now know.

The secret had got out from a child in Year 4. His sister's friend had seen them in Pizza Parlour the other day, and with social media, the gossip had soon spread. It wouldn't take long for the whole school to find out.

As always, Tom was amazing, deflecting any nasty comments like a footballer defending a goal. The teachers all seemed to give Peter sad sympathetic glances as they passed him in the corridor. Mrs Gordan was great. She allowed Peter to stay in at playtime, so he could read the first of the books he had chosen. It was a saga of three books about a group of warrior soldiers going on a long quest to find hidden treasure.

However, she did get angry with him when he lost his patience with the fluffy heads. They had been constantly teasing him and humming the song under their breath. He had had enough and had thrown a rubber across the room at them. It hit Melissa, *smack*, right on the nose. Her scream could have been heard miles away. For this, he got sent to the headmaster's office.

Once again, he was facing Alan across his desk. He noticed the big tin had been moved to the window. *Nothing out of there for me today,* he thought.

"Oh, Peter. It's not been a good day, has it? I know how you feel. They are all talking about me as well. Just try and ignore it. Tomorrow they will gossip about someone else."

Peter couldn't help but blurt out, "How could you possibly know how I feel? Everyone is laughing at me because of you."

"I'm sorry but give it time. You'll have to have a detention for hurting Melissa and I'll have to tell your mum. I'll ring her later, as she's at work now."

Peter's stomach was churning and his heart was pounding in his chest.

"I hate you!" he shouted so loudly that Mr Turner took a small step backwards. He had to get out of there. Without waiting to be dismissed, he opened the door and ran out of the office only to bump straight into Mrs O'Sullivan.

With a steady hand on his shoulder, she guided him to a nearby chair.

"Oh goodness, Peter, you've had a rough day, haven't you? I understand things are tricky for you at the moment. I expect Mr Turner isn't your favourite person. I wonder if I can do anything to help."

Peter looked up into her face. Was she really worried about him or did she just need his help? At this precise moment, he didn't really care.

"Tell you what, it's nearly home time. I am leaving early today so I could give you a lift home. You won't have to worry about anyone teasing you and we can talk about how I can help you cope with Mr Turner."

Peter had to think fast. He knew he shouldn't take lifts with strangers but she was a teacher from school.

At that moment, Mr Turner came out of his office and turned to go up the corridor. Two Year 6 children were walking the other way carrying a large bag of footballs to return to the P.E cupboard. As they saw Peter, they both started to laugh and pretend to blow kisses to him. That helped him to make up his mind. "Yes please, miss. A lift would be great." She arranged to meet him in the staff car park at the end of the day.

He only had time to explain to Tom what was happening, promising to text him later with all the news. He did, however, have to apologise to Melissa, whose nose had a big red mark on it. Begrudgingly he did, even though he protested that she had started it.

The journey home was strange.

Sully's car was a complete contrast to the jeep. It was a small, pale blue mini type car.

Japanese, he thought but didn't really know. It smelt of flowers, and there were stickers on the back window: *Save the planet & I love Cornwall-surfs up.* A box of pink tissues stuck out of the passenger door pocket and a cat-shaped air freshener hung from the mirror. A half empty packet of toffee sat in the cup holder between the front seats.

"So, Peter. How can we make your life better? Mr Turner has messed it up for you, hasn't he? You know people think that he is an outstanding teacher. I think he has just been lucky. The right children, the right questions. It's as if he knew what the questions would be!" She coughed to clear her throat. "Did you know that he used to work for OFSTED."

Peter had heard of OFSTED, but wasn't really sure what they were.

Billy French in Year 6 said they were like school police.

Sully pushed a button on her door and, like magic, her window opened to let in a cool, refreshing breeze. The jeep didn't have any fancy gadgets like that. After a deep breath, she continued, "It's very selfish of him to date your mum and not ask or even tell you about it. It must be awful for you knowing that he could one day maybe become your dad."

What! Peter gulped hard; his mouth had suddenly become very dry. *My dad! No way is that going to happen.*

"I know you don't like him. The sausage trick was excellent. Unfortunate it didn't work." She seemed to laugh quietly under her breath. It reminded him of a cat purring.

"How do you know about that?" Peter wondered how she knew so much about his life.

"I know lots of things, young man. Okay, we're here." The car had stopped at the bottom of his road. He couldn't remember telling her his address but he must have.

"I'll see you tomorrow at school, Peter." She offered him a toffee, which in the warm sunlight had become all sticky. He opened the door, pushed it shut and she drove off, waving as she went. Sucking the toffee slowly, he walked the remaining short distance to his house. He wanted to finish the sweet before he got in, and his mouth was so dry; it disappeared quickly.

He had so much to think over, but first he had to update Tom.

12

As he opened the door, the music playing in the kitchen was a reassuring sound. His mum appeared.

"Alan rang me. I'm sorry you've had a tough day but, to be honest, at least it's out there now. The fuss will all soon blow over and we can get back to normal. I should really ground you for what you did to that girl. But it's completely out of character for you and sounds like she had been teasing you all day. So, I'm going to let it go." She walked forward and gave him a tight, comforting cuddle. It felt amazing and for a while it seemed like everything was okay. After a few seconds, he pulled away and ran upstairs to his room.

Tom had messaged him three times, impatiently wanting to know what had happened. Peter relayed as much of Sully's conversation as he could. Tom asked him exactly what he was wondering himself. What did she want Peter to do? He had no idea but he did know it wasn't going to be easy, and a small part of him was sacred.

He found it difficult to sleep that night. Going over and over everything that had happened. OFSTED seemed to be the key thing, but how? Was Sully implying that Mr Turner knew the questions in advance? Because that was cheating! Eventually, he drifted off to sleep dreaming about Army

Convoy and Mr Turner's jeep had become the main combat vehicle.

The next day, the teasing continued. He didn't go to breakfast club. Somehow, he had lost his appetite. At school, the fluffy heads continued with their silly songs. Although inside he was furious, he managed to contain his anger. At break time, Tobias sidled up to him and slipped five Jaffa cakes into his hand.

"Thought you deserved a treat," he said, winking at him as he walked away. The sweet treat was just what Peter needed. Tom continued to be his bodyguard.

With Roman Day tomorrow, he was practising his defence with a pretend sword and shield. They decided to go up to the library at lunchtime and try and snoop around Sully's room. The pretending Roman armour had made Tom braver than normal.

English was before lunch. Poems again.

The fluffy heads continued with any chance to embarrass Peter, making up silly poems about Peter's mum and Mr Turner. Mrs Gordan had finally had enough. She shouted at them loudly from the front of the classroom to stop now or they would all be split up for the rest of the term. Tom and Peter finally had something to smile at.

13

After gobbling down their lunch, the boys grabbed their reading books and headed upstairs. They were stopped once by a dinner lady but Tom convinced them Peter was still upset about all the teasing and needed some space. This worked, so they carefully and quietly tiptoed down the corridor, past the library to Sully's room.

"Yes, great. I think it's working. If you can let me have the answers tonight. Okay, bye." That was Sully's voice, loud and booming.

Quickly, the boys sat in the library area on the large, comfy cushions and bean bags put there to encourage reading. They pretended to read but were waiting until Sully came out.

"Hello, boys. Good to see you reading so enthusiastically. Mr Jones will be pleased. Peter, can I see you a minute, please? Tom, why don't you go out to play and get some exercise? It's a lovely sunny day. Don't worry I'll look after him."

Tom looked anxiously at his friend, then slowly turned and walked away.

"Did you tell your mum about our chat last night?" Sully was staring carefully at him.

"No," Peter answered truthfully.

"Good. I gather you, like me, want Mr Turner gone. Away from your family. He's ruined everything, hasn't he?" That was a rhetorical question; she didn't want an answer to that question. He had learnt that earlier in a grammar lesson.

She continued, "It's all a front, an act. This school in the top five; it's not how it should be. He knows all the shortcuts as he worked for them. Up to now, no one has questioned it and other schools suffer. No more that will change, and you Peter will help it happen."

Peter had no idea what she was talking about.

"Tomorrow I might have a little task for you. You will be like James Bond, Jason Bourne or even Captain Hudson."

What? She knows about Captain Hudson of Army Convoy. For a brief moment, she was really cool in his eyes. Then she suddenly dismissed him, saying she would find him tomorrow.

Tom, unsurprisingly, hadn't gone far. He was sat on the top step of the stairs. He made Peter repeat everything she said three times. He was completely confused but became excited when Captain Hudson's name was mentioned. Between them, they tried to work out what she might want Peter to do but with no success.

14

The next day, Peter awoke with mixed emotions.

Excited about the Roman workshop, he had been looking forward to this for ages but apprehensive about what Sully would want him to do. For the first time in a couple of days, he wasn't the main topic of conversation. The fluffy heads stole the show today. The costumes that they turned up in looked like something off the TV. Golden headdresses, bangles and leather sandals. They looked more like a girl pop group than Year 5 school children. Most of the class just had an old bed sheet wrapped around themselves.

The class role played how Roman citizens lived. What they would eat, where they lived and what everyone, especially Tom, had been looking forward to, their battle strategy.

The shields and swords they had been making in class now became useful. Half the class made the tortoise formation whilst the other half attacked them with their swords. After 20 minutes, they swapped over. It was supposed to show teamwork. That by linking together, you remained strong but some of the boys got carried away and just wanted to barge into the girls and frighten them. It took Mrs Gordan a few attempts to get everyone to act like disciplined centurions.

The silly girls' costumes were soon ripped, broken and covered in mud. Tom and Peter called this payback.

At the end of the day, just as the class were cleaning up the playground of broken shields, swords and various costumes, Peter saw Sully approaching out the corner of his eye. *Oh no,* he thought. The past few hours had been lovely not having to worry about anything.

"Hello, Peter. Looks like you've had an amazing time. I could see you all from my classroom window. It looked fun. However, it's now time to make your problems disappear. I need your help." Out of her pocket, she pulled a small square-shaped memory card. Peter had seen the teachers use them with their computers. "All I want you to do is put this somewhere in Mr Turner's office out of sight. I know a good place for it."

She paused, looking at him intently. "How about that tin he keeps the rewards in? It's full of lots of little things all different shapes and sizes. Shouldn't be too difficult. Just push it to the bottom under some of the stuff in there. Do it before you go home. That's all you have to do and then it won't be long before your life can go back to normal. Just you and your mum again." With that, she gave Peter a smile and walked away.

Tom had noticed Sully speaking to him and came running over, almost tripping over his torn, dirty sheet, to find out what she wanted.

Peter explained what she wanted him to do.

"Is that all?" Tom exclaimed. "What will that do? Doesn't seem too bad, does it? Are you going to do it?"

Peter's initial instinct was to say no. Something inside him said it was wrong and he might get into trouble. Just at that moment, the silly girls walked past, singing quietly that stupid song again. Peter's anger took over. "That's it. I'm fed up with this. It has to stop. You have to help me. How can we get into his office?"

The boys slowly walked across the playground. The class had been told to go back to class to get changed and to be dismissed. It had to be now.

Suddenly, in a rare moment of brilliance, Tom came up with a plan.

They stood outside the office and, after a few deep breaths of courage, knocked on the door.

15

"Come in." Mr Turner was surprised to see the boys standing there. "Hello, boys, I mean Romans. How can I help?"

Tom's idea was to ask Mr Turner to take a photo of them all dressed up so they could send it to their mums. Mr Turner was delighted to do so. He got them to stand side by side, looking very proud and regal. Luckily for Peter, the big tin was still on the window sill. When Peter had finished posing, he accidently knocked over the tin onto the floor, causing its contents to spill everywhere.

"Oh no. I'm so sorry, sir. I'll pick them all up at once." As he bent down, he turned and winked at his accomplice. Whilst Peter was picking up all the rubbers, pens and stickers, Tom proved really useful by distracting Mr Turner's attention. He asked him loads of questions about his jeep. When did you get it? Why did you choose that jeep? Is it easy to drive? How much was it? With Tom keeping him occupied, Peter reached into his pocket, took out the small black memory card and placed it at the bottom of the big tin. He covered it with all the goodies that had fallen out. He carefully replaced the lid and put the tin back by the window.

"All done, sir. I think we should go now or Mrs Gordan will wonder where we are. Thank you for taking the photo."

Pulling Tom along by his sleeve, Peter almost fell over in his rush to leave the office. Once outside, the boys looked at each other, smiled, high-fived and walked back down to the classroom. Mission accomplished.

The walk home was very quiet. They were both going over everything they had done. What could be on that memory card? What was going to happen next? Neither of them had any answers. After agreeing to text, each other if anything happened the friends parted company arranging to meet as normal in breakfast club.

It was quiet evening. Peter played on his Xbox for an hour after tea, read his book, which he was actually starting to enjoy, and watched TV with his mum. Her favourite programme, celebrity bake off.

Famous people making cakes! He had completely forgotten about school and the memory card until his mum commented that she hadn't heard from Alan tonight and she hoped he was okay.

Peter didn't sleep very well that night. He was worried. What if Mr Turner realised what he done or had found the memory card in the tin. He was having regrets now about helping Sully. Tom had texted several times that evening, asking for news but he had nothing to tell him.

16

Peter's anxiety increased even more the next morning when his mum said she still hadn't heard from Alan and was starting to worry. He set off for school having no idea what the day would bring. He really didn't want to meet Mrs O'Sullivan.

As he arrived at school, he saw a police car parked across the entrance. It was causing lots of interest with everyone wondering what had happened. He ran into breakfast club avoiding the queue for food, heading straight for Tom, who was enjoying a big plate of toast and Marmite. *Yuk,* thought Peter, briefly distracted, *who can eat that stuff?*

"Tom, what's going on? Have you seen the car outside?"

"Yes, it was here when I got in. Haven't seen Mr Turner or Mrs O'Sullivan. What do you think they want? Is it anything to do with us?" Tom put down his toast, suddenly losing his appetite.

Peter's stomach was also starting to churn and he felt a bit lightheaded. The police! He never thought they would become involved.

The morning passed really slowly. Both the boys would glance up every time the classroom door opened. Mrs Gordan told them off several times for not paying attention. Tobias had asked why the police were in school, only to be told to just get on with his work. Then a message came to say that assembly had been cancelled, Even Mrs Gordan was surprised by that.

Just as Peter was starting to relax, another message came to class. Mrs Gordan whispered in his ear that he was needed. Could he go to Mr Turner's office at break time? Peter turned to his friend. Tom gave him a reassuring smile but both of them knew this was not a good thing.

As the other children ran outside to play, Peter slowly and with dread walked down the corridor to the office. Staring at the floor as he crept along, he thought that this was becoming a common event now. He looked up and saw his mum, head bowed, sat on a seat outside the door of the office. Why was she here?

She spoke softly but you could tell she was worried and confused.

"Peter. What's going on? I was called in from work. I think it's something to do with Alan. They said he might be in trouble."

Suddenly, Peter felt a sense of guilt. His mum looked sad and vulnerable and he was now regretting his involvement in Sully's plan. In trying to get at Mr Turner, he had forgotten how it might affect the most important person in his life.

The office door opened and a tall smart policeman appeared.

"Come in, please." He looked at Peter and his mum and beckoned them to follow him.

Once again, Peter was in this office. But this time, it was different.

Behind the desk was a small, fair-haired man wearing large, dark, rimmed glasses. He had a large briefcase open on the desk next to him. Also, beside him was the tin, open.

Oh, blimey! Peter now knew that he was in trouble, but he didn't understand why. The policeman closed the door, sat down on a chair behind him and took out a notebook and pencil. Peter had seen this on the TV. The police wrote down everything.

"Hello, Mrs Saunders and Peter. I'm Mr Blackburn and I'm a senior investigating officer for OFSTED. I'm afraid I'm here to investigate some serious claims against Mr Turner. Cheating and fixing the SAT tests."

Peter gulped hard. He sat deadly still, hoping not to draw attention to himself.

His mum initially shocked and quiet spluttered and almost shouted out, "That's ridiculous. He wouldn't cheat. He loves this school."

The OFSTED man continued that they had had an anonymous call to say that the school was fixing the SATs' results. Giving the Year 6 children knowledge of the questions in advance. That was why the results had been so good recently and why Cameron Street was so high in the school league tables.

After protesting Mr Turner's innocence, his mum turned to look at him. "What has all this got to do with my son? He's 10 years old. Why has he been dragged in here?" Peter had never seen her so strong and protective.

"Well, I was hoping that he could tell us that." Mr Blackburn, the policeman and his mum, all turned towards him, waiting for his reply. The room was silent except for the deep breaths Peter was taking to stop him from panicking and running out of the room. After what seemed a lifetime of silence, Peter couldn't answer even if he wanted to, as his mouth was so dry. Mr Blackburn opened his briefcase and took out a large laptop. He slowly and carefully turned the screen around to face Peter and his mum. With a click of the 'play' button, there on the screen was Tom and Peter dressed in Roman togas. CCTV. How could he have forgotten about that? It was all over school, even in this office. The whole thing was recorded.

The boys having their photo taken, Peter knocking over the tin and then it clearly showed him putting the memory card in and covering it over. Mr Blackburn paused the screen on the image of the memory card in Peter's hand.

"Would you like to explain this?"

17

His mum gasped, "Peter!"

The weeks of emotion suddenly caught up with him. Without hardly taking a breath, he blurted out everything that had happened over the past few weeks. From seeing his mum and head teacher kissing, feeling betrayed and angry, seeing Mrs O'Sullivan in the park, the ride in her car and the conversation they had, being constantly teased and finally the memory card. His mum looked completely baffled and astonished by everything he said.

Now the tears followed. He never cried but today he couldn't stop. Sniffing through the tears, he looked into her teary eyes and whispered, "Sorry, Mum, sorry. I'm so sorry." She replied by pulling him close and giving him the tightest cuddle that was possible without hurting him.

"Oh, Peter, I'm sorry. I didn't realise how this had affected you. My little pumpkin."

Mr Blackburn looked at him, frowning. "Well done for telling the truth. It's what we thought. We have suspected Oakside was up to something. They could never accept being beaten by a school like Cameron Street. As for Mrs O'Sullivan, now we have plenty of evidence against her. I think we should pay her a visit. Surprisingly, she's not in school today! She rang in sick this morning." He turned to the policeman and nodded.

"It was terrible that she used a child in her schemes. You can go now, Peter, but please don't talk to anyone about this."

Holding his mum's hand tightly, Peter left the office so happy to be out of there. Neither of them knew what to say; so much had just happened. Finally, his mum broke the silence. "Let's go home. Come on."

The phone never seemed to stop ringing that evening. The school, Tom's mum, the police. It was endless. Peter tried to text Tom. He hoped he wasn't in too much trouble, but as a punishment, his mum had taken his phone away. She had also stopped him playing on the Xbox.

Just as he was getting ready for bed, he got a call from mum to come downstairs. He pulled his soft fleecy dressing gown comfortingly around him and made his way down to see her.

There in the living stood next to mum was Mr Turner.

Oh God, thought Peter. *I'm for it now.*

He was terrified about how the next few moments would go.

"It's okay, Peter. I'm not really cross with you. You were upset and confused about me seeing your mum, and we didn't deal with that very well. I don't want to replace your dad, but I do love your mum." The look on her face when he said that made Peter feel even guiltier than he did already.

"Mrs O'Sullivan used how you were feeling to get what she wanted and that was very wrong of her. I hope you know that I would never cheat. I don't like the exams but they are always done correctly. We have worked very hard over the past few years to make Cameron Street a good, strong school.

I did work, work for OFSTED, but it was a very long time ago and I was only sorting out all the post for each department. You need to accept me being around because Kathy and I are together, so please accept it."

His mum looked at him pleadingly. He mumbled his reply, saying how sorry he was, in an embarrassed, croaky voice. He was genuinely sorry, and he did want his mum to be happy.

He went to bed but couldn't get to sleep, going over and over the events of the past few weeks. He looked up at his dad's football shirt above his bed, reached up and pulled Tatty bear down off the shelf, giving him a long-awaited cuddle and made a decision.

18

The next day, he had to stay home. He was suspended from school for the rest of the week, which wasn't really a surprise as he knew he deserved it.

His mum also took a day off, and they talked and talked about everything that had happened and about what life with his dad was like before the accident.

That evening, Mr Turner came around for tea. Surprisingly, Peter found that he didn't really mind.

Apparently, the police had found Mrs O'Sullivan and she had been arrested. Oakside School was also under investigation, in case other people knew about her scheme. They were still trying to identify the man in the van. Tom had got away with only a couple of detentions for his role in it all, and they wouldn't be allowed to meet up for a few days.

Over tea, Peter looked at the two adults. They were happy and smiling. *I suppose I could get used to this,* he thought. The decision he had made was to give Alan a chance. After all, he did support United.

Mr Turner turned to face him.

"Well, Peter. This time next year, it's your turn for the SATs."

The three of them looked at one another and, after a brief pause, they suddenly started to laugh.